Cornish
Bal Maidens

JOYCE.

For further information of all the titles in this series please visit:-
www.tormark.co.uk

Designed by Alix Wood, www.alixwood.co.uk

Published by Tor Mark, United Downs Ind Est, Redruth, Cornwall TR16 5HY
First published 2010

ISBN 978 085025 420 4

Printed by R Booth Ltd, The Praze, Penryn, Cornwall TR10 8AA

Dolcoath Copper Mine in 1831. (Painting by T Allom in Royal Cornwall Museum) Bal maids carrying out a number of tasks, including spalling, cobbing and bucking the ore in preparation for sampling

Cover: Dolcoath Mine, Camborne at the turn of the 20th century. The maidens of various ages wore a variety of hats, but all sport clean, white aprons. They were engaged in shovelling broken rock (Tony Clarke)

Title page: An old Redruth bal maid called 'Joyce' (Paddy Bradley)

INTRODUCTION

The Cornish metal mining industry probably goes back to the Early Bronze Age, perhaps for 4,000 years, and it seems fairly certain that during much of that time women worked alongside their menfolk in the industry. In Cornwall the generic term for a female surface mine worker is 'bal maiden' or 'bal maid', 'bal' originally being a Cornish word for a group of tinbounds or workings, and later applied to any Cornish mine. The expression really came into use during the copper boom, which started at the end of the seventeenth century, and lasted until the near collapse of the industry in the 1860s. Copper dressing was extremely labour-intensive, and the surface areas around Cornwall's many hundred copper mines were filled with thousands of bal maidens, carrying out a number of tasks, most of them unskilled. Thereafter, the term was applied to the diminishing group of women who worked on the dressing floors of the surviving tin mines and in the tin streams which occupied most of the valleys of west Cornwall. The earliest records of these women are from the thirteenth and fourteenth century lead-silver mines on the Cornish-Devon border. The female mine workers next appear in the records of the early eighteenth century tin and copper mines of west Cornwall, and thereafter there are numerous references and descriptions of them. Their last appearance seems to have been at Geevor Tin Mine, during the Second World War, where they were employed on the conveyor belts, picking unwanted rubbish from the ore flowing into the tin mill.

THE GWENNAP BAL MAID'S CHANT

I can buddy, and I can rocky,
And I can walk like a man,
I can looby and shaky,
And please the old Jan.

These dialect words for the ore dressing processes carried out by bal maidens refer to 'buddling' (buddy), breaking rocks or 'spalling' (rocky), 'treloobing' (looby), washing the waste fines from the ore, and 'riddling' or 'griddling', which involved shaking a sieve to remove smaller, unwanted particles.

MEDIEVAL BAL MAIDENS

The activities of the royal medieval lead-silver mines at Bere Alston, on the Devon side of the Tamar River, are well documented. The recruitment of miners and other skilled workers from all over the realm; the names and professions of those workers; the wages paid; the materials supplied to the mines; in fact all the details of costs and personnel are to be found in those ancient records. With these details are also the names and activities of some of the female mine workers – the bal maidens. The ore crushing plant, dressing floors, blacksmith's shop, smelting furnaces and refining arrangements were all at Calstock, on the Cornish side of the river, and it was there that these women and girls were employed.

Let us look at the names of some of these women. Agnes Oppehulle, Isabelle Cutard, Gunhild daughter of Bon, Dyonisia, Desiderata and Agnes de Milleton, Emma de Fallyng, Matilda Bate, Mansoe Bogge, Joanna Cole, and Agnes Sludde The tasks these women carried out were typical of the work carried out by bal maids throughout the ages. 'Washing black ore', was what most of them did at the mine. The ore mined at Bere Alston was galena, which contained mostly lead, but was principally being worked for its silver content. The bal maids were cleaning unwanted gangue (waste material) from the ore prior to crushing – and sometimes also after it was crushed. Another task less frequently carried out by the women was 'washing refinery ash'. This refinery ash was mostly bone ash, used as a flux (material used to assist separation) during the refining process, when silver was separated from the lead, which had already been smelted. Ash was purchased in large quantities by the mine from as far away as Exeter, where the many slaughter houses would have had facilities for gathering bones to be sold for several purposes, including burning for the resultant ash. The accounts also show the women and girls doing general labouring around the mine, such as 'cutting reeds for a store for refinery ash'.

Bal maidens were employed as casual labour, and although some of them, like Agness Oppehulle, Isabelle Cutard and Emma de Fallyng, were employed fairly constantly, most of the others seem to have come and gone as required. The usual working week appears to have been either five or six days, again depending on demand, and the daily pay for an adult bal maiden was one penny. Their young female assistants were paid either two-thirds of a penny, or a half-penny a day. Another assistant ore dresser was a young lad, Richard le Worere, who was also paid at the lower rate.

Who were these bal maidens and where did they come from? As noted above, the miners and other skilled men were recruited from Wales, Derbyshire, the Forest of Dean, Mendip and from all over Cornwall and Devon. Although some of these women and girls undoubtedly were local, several appear to have come to the mine with their menfolk. Matilda Bate was probably either the wife or daughter of Richard Bate, a smelter. Dyonisia, Agnes and Desiderata de Milleton were almost certainly related to Edmund de Milleton, a refinery assistant. Joanna Cole would have been the wife or daughter of John Cole a mine chandler and Agnes Sludde was very likely married or otherwise related to Richard Sludde, a Calstock blacksmith. The lad, Richard le Worere, could have been the son of William le Worere, a furnaceman.

A Framing Girl, or Racker, in Tin Mine.

Bal maiden operating a tin slime frame or rack. The picture is dated November 9th 1850 (Paddy Bradley)

There are many sources of information on the tin mines and tin streams operating during the medieval period, but despite these detailed records, there do not appear to be any written references to women working in them. For example, in the legal case involving Abraham the Tinner, which went before the Duke of Cornwall's court in 1357, and heard detailed facts about his several tin streams and mines, there is no mention of female labour there, only a reference to the fact that 'he has been working with 300 men in the king and prince's mine for their profit'. None of the many hundred tinbound registrations from the reigns of Henry VII and Henry VIII contain the names of female tinners, and neither does the detailed study of the sixteenth century Cornish tin industry written by Thomas Beare. Both Richard Carew and John Norden, in their late-sixteenth century descriptions of the Cornish mining industry, fail to mention female mine workers. The Philosophical Transactions of the Royal Society, started after the

Botallack in the 1860s. This early picture by the Penzance photographer, Gibson, shows the tin dressing floors along the top of the cliffs. Several bal maidens have paused from work to be photographed. The Crowns engine houses can be seen in the background (Tony Clarke)

Bal maidens using cobbing hammers to knock unwanted waste from good copper ore. Note they are seated and a hand barrow is shown (James Henderson, *On The Methods Generally Adopted in Cornwall in Dressing Tin & Copper Ores*, 1858)

Restoration of 1660, carried several detailed descriptions of mining and mining practice, but there is no mention of women and girls working in the Cornish tin mining industry.

Although women were not working tinners, by the seventeenth century, with the gentry controlling the stannaries, both male and female landowners and mineral lords owned whole groups of tinbounds on their land. Their tollers (landowner's agents) renewed these bounds annually, to keep ownership in house. Two such women, both widows who had inherited their husband's property, were Thomasyn Coryn and Jane Gully. They both owned bounds in St Agnes and Kenwyn parishes. Mrs Coryn held all or part of some fifteen bounds in Creegbrawse and Killifreth, in 1639, and Mrs Gully held bounds in St Agnes, Gwennap and Kenwyn.

And so, after that brief but surprisingly detailed record of those bal maidens of seven centuries ago, these stalwart women disappear into the ether, before re-emerging in great numbers and in clear outline at the beginning of the eighteenth century.

THE EIGHTEENTH CENTURY BAL MAID

The modern bal maiden's appearance on the mining scene in great numbers and as an essential part of the burgeoning Cornish copper mining industry, had its roots outside the county. Although by the end of the seventeenth century, as William Pryce (*Mineralogia Cornubiensis*, 1778) has pointed out, women and girls were becoming involved in the dressing of the tin tailings (waste), which came from the hundreds of tin mines in Cornwall, it was copper mining which was to see bal maidens employed on a large scale. The increasing demand for Cornish copper, which was underway by the 1690s, was fuelled by the expanding manufacturing industry of the English Midlands. Outside entrepreneurs, like John Coster and Gabriel Wayne, were not only acting as agents for Gloucestershire copper smelters and brass makers, but they were becoming adventurers in the mines themselves. They were organising the fleets of ships to carry the ore to Gloucestershire and arranging for the copper metal and brass to be sold to the factories of Birmingham and elsewhere. They also brought with them new attitudes to organisation of industry, which increasingly involved the use of female and child labour.

THE BAL MAIDENS ON WORK DAYS.

THE BAL MAIDEN ON SUNDAY.

Illustrations of bal maidens on work days and dressed up in their finery on Sundays (Royal Cornwall Museum)

The rather attractive picture painted by Pryce, of young girls and boys *'moving up and down in the buddles, to separate the Tin from the refuse, with naked feet like the ancient Dancers'*, or *'lappiors'*, seems far removed from the new situation. From the 1720s onward whole communities of Cornish women were involved in copper dressing, and it is from that time that the picture of the traditional Cornish bal maid makes her appearance. Among the earliest extant Cornish mine cost books are those of Pool Adit and Penhellick Work, which start in 1711. John Coster, the copper entrepreneur was involved in the mine, and his interest was in the copper there, although up until the beginning of the eighteenth century the small mines which were to make up Pool Adit were all tin mines. By the end of the 1720s copper ore was being produced at an impressive rate, and local women were being taken on as 'peekers' or pickers. They were employed to 'pick' the good ore from the bad. It is appropriate that Pool Adit should provide the earliest evidence of bal maids, because the mine was the great success story of the first half of the eighteenth century. Even more than Dolcoath, Pool Adit made the fortune of the Basset family, furnishing them with over £10,000 annual profit for many years.

Analysis of the cost book entries makes interesting reading. In October 1729 there were 28 'peekers' employed on Pool Adit's copper floors. These floors lay along the south side of Trevenson, between the main entrance to Cornwall College and Tolvaddon Road. Three of these pickers were male, and were probably young lads, and all of them, male and female, were paid at a rate of 4d a day. Sixteen of the women and three of the males worked 20 days in the month, which suggests a 'normal' four day week. The average number of days worked was 19 days, with three people only working 15 days.

The April 1730 entry shows the pickers had increased to 34 as the mine production increased, and this included four males. All were paid 4d a day. Ten of the ore dressers worked 20 days and 11, 18 days. The average was 16 days in the month. Five of these pickers, including one male, only worked nine days in the month. By August 1731, copper output had increased significantly and 60 pickers were employed, made up of 55 females and five males. The number of days also increased dramatically, with 41 women and four boys working 23 days in the

HAZARDS & ACCIDENTS

The 19th century industrial scene was inherently dangerous. Wherever young women sought work there were potential dangers and none more so than when the industries were connected to mining. Ancillary industries, like gunpowder manufacture and safety fuse making, carried risks we today would consider unacceptable. The safety fuse factories around west Cornwall witnessed a spate of disastrous accidents in the second half of the 19th century, with young women being killed in explosions at an alarming rate. In 1861 and 1865 at fuse factories in Pool two explosions of gunpowder killed a total of four female workers. In the modern, safety conscious Bickford-Smith fuse factory at Tuckingmill, eight girls were killed when gunpowder ignited in 1872, and in the Unity Fuse Works, St Day, another factory designed with safety in mind, five women, between the ages of 14 and 37 years, were killed in similar circumstances in 1875.

Explosions of mine boilers also caused death among girls employed there. In the winter of 1830, at United Hills Mine, several workers, including a 20 year old bal maiden, called Elizabeth Goyne, were warming themselves in the boilerhouse when the boiler exploded. Among the dead was young Elizabeth. In 1858 at Boiling Well Mine, near Hayle, a boiler explosion claimed the life of another bal maiden sheltering in the building for warmth.

Machinery on the dressing floors of the tin and copper mines also represented potential hazards for the workforce, and not infrequently did it prove fatal for surface workers. The tragic story of Eliza Jane Hall, who was a bal maiden at Ding Dong Mine, high on the moorlands of West Penwith, illustrates this. During a break her friend, Alice Ann Stevens went to collect water from a nearby stream, whilst Eliza Jane, despite the shouted warning of her friend, climbed onto the big crown gear wheel of the winding engine, which was not in motion. She got off it, but when the bell sounded that it was to restart, she climbed back on, shouting 'I will go round!' She thought it would be fun to ride it like a roundabout. Unfortunately, her clothes caught in the gearing and she was dragged to the ground screaming. The whim-driver immediately stopped the engine, but it was too late for her body was torn almost into pieces, with some parts entangled in the machinery. She died some time later. Another tragedy occurred at the Magor Tin Streams, on the Red River near Camborne, in January 1888. A young bal maiden got too close to the unprotected shaft of the stamps waterwheel. Her dress caught in the shaft and she was dragged into the stamps and crushed to death.

There were also miraculous escapes by bal maidens from highly dangerous situations. In August 1858 at Porkellis United Mines, in Wendron, a quarter acre of ground sank beneath the dressing floors for a depth of between 9m and 12m. With a noise like thunder the dressing floors collapsed into the mine, carrying with it a dozen tin dressing frames, tended by several bal maidens. Miraculously, they all escaped without serious injury, although deep beneath their feet six men and a boy were entombed. Fifty miners survived the disaster.

The women and girls employed in the mines and ancillary industries of Cornwall understood the dangers inherent in their work, and like the men of the time, they stoically accepted them and got on with their lives.

A group of Camborne bal maidens at the end of the 19th century. All are wearing the traditional 'gook' head dress and clean white aprons, suggesting that they had been warned that a photographer was to be present. They are using long-handles shovels (Bennetts of Camborne: courtesy of The Cornwall Centre)

month. Fifty-two ore dressers worked between 22 and 26 days during the month. One or two only did 11 or 12 days in the month, but it seems that most pickers were working at least a four day week.

What can be learned from this about the way they worked? Several of these ore pickers were regularly employed by the mine, and the most regular also tended to work more days than the more casual. Let us take five examples. Susan Dorman worked 20 days in October 1729, 18 in April 1730 and 23 days in August 1731. Mary Ninnis did 20, 18 and 22 days; Mary Pearce worked 20, 18 and 23 days; Jane Wills 18, 14 and 23 days, and Ann Nettle worked 20, 20 and 23 days, respectively.

The same daily rate was paid at Cooks Kitchen Mine, just to the south of Pool Adit. This rapidly expanding former tin mine was becoming a very important copper mine and by the middle of the century its workforce, including bal maids, was increasing. The October 1766 cost book tells us that 38 bal maidens worked an average of 22 days in the month for 4d a day. All the ore pickers in these two mines, whether male or female, regular or occasional, old or young, experienced or not, received the same daily wage rate. They were all casual day labourers, who would have been taken on and discharged as needed by the mine.

The next case to look at is that of New Dolcoath, in Camborne. By the 1760s it was the largest and most productive of all eighteenth century Cornish copper mines. The mine pay books for the years 1771 to 1791 tend to lump all the ore dressers into one large group called 'pickers and cobbers'. No individual names of these women were usually given, although some bal maidens' names appear when they worked at the copper furnace. The total number of 'pickers and cobbers' can only be guessed at by reference to the total wage bill. The January 1772 entry in the pay book indicates that these women were paid 6d a day. The wage bill came to £111 2s 3d, and if we assume that the average number of days worked by these women was 20 days in the month, then the number employed on the copper dressing floors would have been about 222.

West Wheal Seton, Camborne. Late 19th century picture of several bal maids pausing from their work. Two, on the extreme right are carrying a hand barrow (Tony Clarke)

Only three of the bal maids employed at the copper furnace were named: Ann Heather, Sarah Harrise and Mary Osbron (Osborne). Ann Heather was paid £1 13s 1d for herself and partners. At 6d a day that represented 66 days work, which suggests that three or four women were involved. Sarah Harrise was paid 6d for one day's work and Mary Osbron was paid 1s 8d, presumably for something like 3 days. None of these women signed their names for their wages, all making their mark, 'x'.

In the summer of 1788 the copper price had gone too low for Dolcoath to continue. As she was run down following the stopping of her pumps and the gradual abandonment of the underground workings, activity continued at surface to pick over the 'halvans' or low grade ore left on surface. In Dolcoath's Halvan Cost Book, under the date of August 1789, an entry has: "Sarah Michell Attendance on Wey'g etc – 1s 6d." Weighing the low-grade copper ore prior to selling it to the smelters was a fairly responsible job. Sarah was clearly not your

West Wheal Frances, Illogan, in the 1890s. Nine bal maids of various ages posing beside a ragging frame for tin dressing. (Bennetts of Camborne: courtesy of The Cornwall Centre)

average 'run of the mill' bal maiden, and her case raises the question as to what other types of work female mine workers might have been engaged in during the eighteenth century.

Poldice, in Gwennap, was a very important and very ancient mine. In the early sixteenth century it had been a significant tin mine. By the time of the eighteenth century copper boom, Poldice was producing impressive tonnages of copper ore, and was among the biggest mines in the large Gwennap mining district. Entries in the cost book for May 1798 to February 1799 refer to two women who were paid a regular monthly salary, presumably for supervising the other bal maidens at Poldice. Every month Ann Bray was paid 6s and Jane Wasley 10s 6d. The only exceptions were in June 1708, when Wasley was paid an extra 4d, to celebrate 'midsummer', and in November, when her salary was

12s instead of the regular 10s 6d. What is interesting is that neither woman was a 'casual' worker, and Jane Wasley appears to have been regarded as being on the establishment, in that she was paid 4d for the midsummer celebrations.

Another example is that of Wheal Towan for the period January to April 1784. In contrast to the previous examples, this copper mine was operating on a very small scale at the time. Seven bal maidens worked there and their wages were between 4d and 6d a day. In April Grace Cockin worked 19 days for 6d a day, and earned 9s 9d. Elizabeth Nancarrow worked eight days for 5d a day, Phebe Nancarrow worked nine days for 5d a day, Jane Foss worked nine days for 5d a day, Mary Ead worked six days for 6d a day and Agnes Nettle worked 12 days at 5d. In the January-February account Grace Cockin earned 6d a day, Phebe Nancarrow 5d, Elizabeth Nancarrow 4d and Charity Tonkin 4d. We do not know why Elizabeth Nancarrow's rate was 4d in January and February and 5d in April. Perhaps she was performing a different task, and the pay rates might have varied for different jobs. Thomas Tonkin, who worked with these women, and may have been the ore dresser in charge, was paid 1s a day. These bal maids averaged 10 days a month, with only Grace Cockin seeming to have been a more regular employee, at 19 days.

It is apparent that in each of these cases the bal maidens were casual, relatively low-paid workers. Every example is of a 'day rate' worker. There is no evidence of these ore dressers ('pickers & cobbers') being employed as piece workers. They were regarded as unskilled day labourers, who could be taken on or discharged at a moments' notice.

William Pryce in *Mineralogia Cornubiensis*, published in 1778, described the manner of dressing and cleansing copper ore in the mid-eighteenth century, and his description explains why, when bal maidens first appeared in any numbers in the 1720s, they were merely called 'pickers', and by the end of the century they were more usually called 'pickers & cobbers'. *Good Copper is commonly dug and raised in large masses, as little mixed with any thing else as possible, a great part of it is solid Ore that needs no washing. When it comes to grass they make a* sortment of the larger stones from the smaller, and spal or break them to a less size, throwing aside the poorer part, which is afterwards to be streked and washed. But when the Ore rises plentifully, and with little waste, it may perhaps be a loss and detriment to wash it; and, if it come moderately dry, a person near the shaft where it rises, lifts it in a Griddle, or iron sieve, of one inch meash (mesh) or less. The part that runs through the griddle, if not clean enough for sale, is washed; and it is seldom that griddled or small Ore is so pure and clean as not to require washing. The poor or smaller Ore is generally carried to the streke or strakes, sometimes after being griddled…

The streke or strake is made of two deal boards laid flat for a bottom fourteen inches in the ground, on an inclined plane, with two sides formed of one deal board each, resembling a narrow shallow chest without a cover. In this runs a pretty quick stream of water. One person throws the foul Ore into the streke, while another moves and tosses it

Providence Mine, St Ives, in the late 19th century. Several bal maidens can be seen posing beside the tin slime frames they were working on (Paddy Bradley)

16

with a shovel in the stream, by which means the slimy earthy parts are carried by the water into a slime pit just below; and the stony coarse poorer part settles in great measure on the tail or lower end of the boards, which at times is divided, and cast aside to be stamped, as it contains some Ore.

Pryce then refers to the part the bal maidens play in this process: *The largest stones, either of Ore or waste, rise uppermost by the motion of the shovel; these the dresser throws on one side of the streke, where women and children sit to pick out the good stones of Ore, and from thence called Pickers. The remainder is laid by to be Bucked, or broke smaller with flat iron hammers made for the purpose.* This explains why, when bal maidens first appear in the ore dressing process, they are generally merely referred to as pickers ('peekers'). By the last decades of the eighteenth century these bal maidens were also being called 'cobbers', and Pryce describes the task which gave them the name. *The picked Ore, which is rich and solid, is put to a number of girls called Cobbers, who break it on large stones with flat polled hammers to the size of a chestnut and less, and it is then called Cobbed Ore.*

THE NINETEENTH CENTURY BAL MAIDEN

By 1800, with the end of low copper prices due to the demise of the North Wales mines, the Cornish industry picked up and moved forward again. However, this time things were to be different. Cornish engineers were modifying, innovating and inventing new engines and better techniques, and the revived mines were being organised on an industrial scale. Improved organisation of labour was one area where things changed, and the attitude which viewed female surface labourers as mere 'pickers and cobbers', was replaced by a more intelligent use of their labour. This did not mean that they became piece workers, or were part of some imagined 'tribute team', for they were to remain as casual labour, paid by the day, and they could still be hired and fired at will. However, although they were not piece workers, they did have a quota of work to complete in order to get their daily rate of so much a day. But what changed was that the variety of tasks assigned to them expanded considerably. They were viewed as more versatile than they had been.

The basic tasks carried out by the ore dressers did not change materially from the time of Pryce, in the 1760s and 1770s. What did

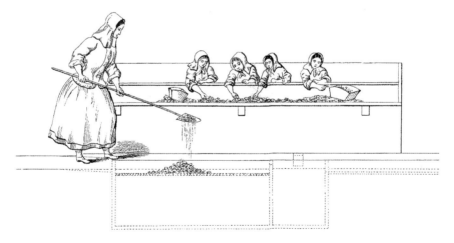

Bal maidens picking out the good copper ore from the waste. This task was usually done by the very young bal maidens and was considered light work (Henderson)

Tincroft Mine, Illogan in the late 19th century. A bal maid is spalling rocks, which are being shovelled onto a cart (Bennetts of Camborne: courtesy of The Cornwall Centre)

change was that bal maids were involved in more of these tasks. 'Ragging', that is reducing large rocks of ore to manageable size by the use of 14lb sledge or ragging hammers, was done by young men. 'Riddling' or 'griddling' was the next process, and girls of about 16 years of age performed this task. It consisted of using a sieve-like apparatus with an inch mesh to sort the ore. Next, girls of about the same age used a 5-7lb 'spalling hammer' to reduce the ore to fist size. Girls of about 15 years then used a 'cobbing hammer' to break away the ore from unwanted gangue material. This hammer had a long head which curved forward rather than backward, as with a pick. Finally, the ore-bearing rock was subject to 'bucking'. This was better paid than the other tasks and was reserved for the more experienced maidens, who could earn up to a shilling a day by mid-century. A square-headed, flat-faced hammer was used by the bucker, who placed gravel-size rock on a metal plate called an 'anvil'. The 'bucker' held her hammer with two hands, striking and grinding the gravel in one fairly deft movement. Other tasks carried out by these bal maidens were shifting the broken ore around the floors with hand or wheel barrows, and general labouring.

The modern view of those nineteenth century bal maids is undoubtedly coloured by the comments of educated observers of the time. Men like George Henwood, for example, who, although rising from humble beginnings, nevertheless took a rather superior, middle-class and patronising view of these working women. He viewed them through a very jaundiced eye, regarding them as usually dirty, foul-mouthed and shallow, as he tended to see all the working classes. He wrote (*Cornwall's Mines and Miners*) that due to working alongside men, these bal maids had a want of modesty and delicacy. Long hours away from home whilst performing manual labour, rendered them unfit for domestic duties, so that when they married, their husbands were

Dolcoath Mine, Camborne at the end of the 19th century. These tin dressing slime frames were situated in the Red River valley between Tuckingmill and Brea Village. Scores of bal maidens were employed there in the late 19th century (Tony Clarke)

HAND FRAME

Bal maidens using manually operated hand frames or racks to separate the tin from the lighter waste material (Henderson)

driven to the pub from their comfortless homes. He tells of two women who stood in for unavailable men at the copper weighing, and described the excessive labour they endured, while being taunted and cheered on by the raucous comments of the men who watched them sweating and struggling. Bal maids were subject to considerable 'coarse joking' and 'rude behaviour' by their male workmates, and Henwood considered it particularly bad that these girls often had to eat their food with the men. He was pleased that some bigger and better-run mines provided separate eating areas for the sexes.

Henwood said girls usually started on the dressing floors when they were only six or seven years old, and over the years gradually learned to carry out all the tasks which bal maidens performed. Whilst working they were constantly exposed to the cold and wet, and this had a deleterious affect upon their long-term health. However, he wrote that this was not the worst effect of their work:

The hard work is not the greatest calamity of which we complain,

Basset Mines, Illogan at the end of the 19th century. A group of tin dressers, four of whom are bal maids. Round convex buddles were just being installed there (Tony Clarke)

that is a mere physical evil; what we most deplore is, that when called upon to take upon themselves the duties of wife and mother, they are totally unfit for them. How can the moral standard of society amongst the lower orders be raised by mothers and sisters with such education and examples? It is utterly hopeless. Taken from their hearths at so early an age, and kept at work for ten hours per day, they have little opportunity, and less inclination, to attend to the domestic and matronly duties so necessary for their future culture, and well-being. Their being associated in such numbers, and before men, a spirit of rivalry in dress (perhaps inherent in all women) is soon engendered, and every attention – all their thoughts and earnings – are devoted to this method of making themselves attractive. To see the 'bal maidens' on a Sunday, when fully dressed, would astonish a stranger; whilst at their work the pendant earrings and showy bead necklaces excite the pity as well as the surprise of the thoughtful. All desire to save a few shillings for afterlife is discarded, and nothing but display thought of. This is carried on to an incredible extent, and all the preaching in the world will never interfere with the wearing a fine bonnet or shawl, or an attempt to imitate the fashions of their superiors. Rivalry is the order of the day, and thus many are led into temptations. We see no present remedy for this evil, but trusting machinery, and the non-employment of boys underground, may produce a mighty change, and oblige those who ought to be employed in domestic duties to be so engaged to their own honour, their husband's comfort, and their children's blessing.

What the smug Henwood ignored were the needs of the working poor. Going to work was not an option – they were poor – they had no choice! A far more sympathetic and discerning view of bal maidens was expressed by Dr A K Hamilton Jenkin, in his seminal work *The Cornish Miner*. He wrote: *The Cornish bal maidens formed a class of*

The end of the 19th century. A large group a Camborne bal maidens are spalling and shovelling tin ore. (Bennetts of Camborne: courtesy of The Cornwall Centre)

workwomen to themselves, a class, as a whole, shrewd, honest, respectable, and hard-working. Though sometimes rough in speech and generally plain-spoken enough in repartee, as anyone who addressed them disrespectfully soon found, their work brought with it no demoralisation of character. In their dress, too, they were clean and neat, and generally very particular about their appearance. Dr Jenkin then quoted the 1842 Parliamentary Commissioner's report on the employment of children in the mines: They wrap their legs in woollen bands in winter, and in summer many of them envelop their faces and throats in handkerchiefs to prevent them getting sunburnt, whilst on Sundays and holidays they appear in apparel of a showy and often expensive description. The 'gook', seen on many photographs of bal maidens in the later nineteenth century, was worn to keep the sun off their heads, and protruded forward to shade their faces. They also wore what they jokingly called a 'yard of cardboard', which covered the head, neck and face, and was kept in place by a 'curtain' of thin cloth.

The Cornish love to sing, and their long association with Methodism and its tradition of beautiful community hymn singing, encouraged and helped them to practise their singing. In mourning the loss of the bal maidens to Cornwall, Dr Hamilton Jenkin wrote: Their disappearance has robbed the surface of a Cornish mine of one of its most picturesque and characteristic features; and never again, one supposes, will the sound of them going by singing at six o'clock in the summer mornings be heard in the mining areas.

Interesting as these two contrasting views are, there exists a far more revealing account of the lives of Cornish bal maidens. In the Day & Night Book of two Dolcoath mine captains, we find a genuinely unselfconscious description of these working women and girls. Throughout history, mine captains, upon finishing their shift, left notes for the captains who were to follow them. These told of what had been done, what needed doing, where problems lay and what gear was needed. They described disputes between miners, between managers and between bal maidens. They described the work done, the problems encountered, the effect of the weather on surface workers, and the thieving and fiddling which was carried out by some of the miners and

HOW MANY BAL MAIDS WERE THERE?

One area which finds little agreement among historians concerns the number of bal maidens employed. We know that there were considerable numbers and that they tended to increase or decrease with the varying fortunes of the mines, but the figures produced by various observers for the years between the 1780s and the 1840s do not fill us with much confidence. John Rowe (*Cornwall in the Age of the Industrial Revolution*) gives a total of 1,200 to 1,800 for 1787, John Vivian (see above) gives 4,000 to 5,000 women and boys for 1799, Spackman (JR Leifchild, *Cornwall, Its Mines and Miners*) gives 2,098 bal maids in copper mines and 130 in tin mines for 1827 and Sir Charles Lemon (R Burt, *Cornish Mining*) gives 4,414 for 1836. These are at best only educated guesses. Census returns from mining parishes, Parliamentary Commissioner's reports and other sources of material for the decades between 1840 and 1890 are equally vague and give figures as low as 4,135 in 1841 and as high as 14,400 in 1843. Of one thing there is no doubt: thousands of bal maids worked alongside the ore dressers in hundreds of mines from the 1720s to the end of the nineteenth century. In the 1860s more than 2,500 bal maids were working within five miles of Camborne. At the peak of copper mining, in the 1850s and 1860s, between 15 and 20 percent of all mine workers were female, although the percentage was far lower in the less labour intensive tin mills.

not a few of the bal maidens. The journal of captains James Thomas and William Petherick spoke of much more, and one subject which was touched on constantly during the ten months covered by the journal, was that of the bal maidens.

Captain William Petherick wrote of the bal maidens preoccupation with clothes: *the new goods* in the local shops, *new frills, frocks, skirts, shifts, stockings, ell wide, sown print, fast colour, wash to a rag, make up the subject of their discourse.* He wrote of their simple pleasure in small things. *The bal maid enjoys herself more with an ell wide frock, than the peeress does when covered with the diamonds of Golconda at*

Dolcoath Mine, Camborne in the late 19th century. One bal maiden can be seen with a spalling hammer and another with a long-handled 'Cornish shovel' (Bennetts of Camborne: Tony Clarke)

a royal leveee. He referred to the funeral of a young miner, probably killed at Dolcoath. He wrote that there was an *immense concourse of people present & I believe 2 or 3 females to 1 male according to custom* and enquires about *all the business so far as it concerns frocks, frills, bonnets, stockings, garters, etc. Who the mourners were, who was leading & who was not, who was in a fine deal of trouble* (weeping) *& who seemed to take very little notice of it.* A funeral was a fine chance to display the finery the bal maids had spent their meagre cash surplus on – not an opportunity to miss!

Another widely-reported characteristic of these maidens was their often outrageous humour. On December 18th 1822 Petherick wrote: *The samplers were here today ... Mr Noel and Mr Provis ... Mr Provis was desired to put a little snuff on a certain part, by some of our maidens for a very particular purpose.* No prudery there. These bal maids had the ability to make self-important, middle class copper agents a trifle nervous. Despite these suggestions by *some of our maidens*, Petherick reported that generally, *our maidens ... behaved well all throughout the mine today*. This tells us that although some of these women and girls could be crude and outrageous the majority *behaved well*, which warns against generalisations based upon the actions of a few. However, even the Wesleyan local preacher, Captain James Thomas, thought the behaviour of these rowdier girls amusing, and asked *why Mr Provis was desired to put a little snuff on a certain part, by our respectable maidens?* The humour of these bal maidens, although condemned by the self-righteous Henwood and others, was clearly not regarded as unacceptable by all decent and respectable members of society.

Bal maidens bucking the copper ore. Older, more experienced girls usually did this job, which was considered more skilful and generally paid more. The gravel size ore was reduced by a striking and grinding movement, the maids usually held the bucking hammer with both hands (Henderson)

Pednadrea Mine, Redruth toward the end of the 19th century. A group of bal maids pose close to the massive base of the mine's main stack, the lower part of which remains as a landmark at the top of the town. The maidens are wearing the 'gook' and clean aprons for the picture. Note the large, horse-drawn wagons full of rock (Paddy Bradley)

Not all bal maidens were particularly honest, and given the widespread poverty of the working classes, it is hardly surprising that some fell victim to temptation. The Day & Night Book is peppered with references to thieving or fiddling by various bal maids, and the accounts are very revealing. The journal entry for the night of April 23rd 1823 is graphic: *Soon after 6 o'clock tonight I observed 5 or 6 maidens here loitering about until at length they went in Spargoe's cobbing house & I saw them tumbling about something, which I could not find out exactly, but on getting a little closer to the window one of them spied me & gave the alarm. Presently, they all came out & ran away under the account house. I went in the bedroom,* (the count house had all the facilities of a normal house) *but could not see them, so I concluded they were gone in the room. I stayed a minute or so & then went out. I walked on pretty quick & when I came by Bartle's picking tables I saw a girl, whom I knew to be Grace Mayne, standing sentry. On my asking her what she was doing there, she said she was waiting for some one or other to come up from underground. I charged her with stealing barrows & anvils, which she denied. Thinking the others were not far off, I walked into the room & was not surprised to see two girls coming down the house very deliberately with an anvil in a new hand barrow marked T.R.13. I thought to have caught the foremost – but they dropt the barrow on seeing me ... I walked this pare down as far as the fire stamps & then ... saw a girl lugging an anvil under her cloak ... Now all the maidens work at North Roskeere & I think 'twould be necessary for you to enquire into it a little & spale* (fine) *them.*

In June, Petherick enjoined his colleagues to watch out for bal maidens thieving by night, but in July there was another case of thieving by a North Roskear bal maiden. This time an anvil was stolen from the Wheal Susan section of Dolcoath, and Captain Petherick gave the bal maid the chance to return it, failing which she was to be reported to Captain Joseph Vivian, manager of North Roskear. In August several bal maids were involved in stealing a valuable 'whim rope', and Petherick threatened to fire them all if they did not reveal the culprit. They stuck together and were consequently all fired. One of their number, a Miss Pascoe with surprising nerve, immediately got a job at the other end of the mine. Petherick was furious: *I went to take down the maidens' days this afternoon & was very much surprised to find Pascoe's daughter working with Dick Thomas & pare* (small team of workers). *On my questioning her how she got there, she told me one of you had given her leave to go to work, and Capt Rule didn't say that she should not go to work at all. I told her, I should not put down her days until I knew whether Capt Rule & you had given her leave or not. If she has had leave to go to work now, I think the best way will be to pay for some one to steal the rope for her & not put us to the trouble of discharging her again for such a short period.* Captain Thomas replied that he had given her permission to seek work with Dick Thomas if the manager agreed – *so I thought no more about her.*

These cases tells us a lot about the attitudes of the bal maids of the time. The self-confidence and even defiant arrogance displayed by Mayne and Pascoe, not to mention the several others involved, is impressive. They were not intimidated by authority, even though conviction for stealing could land them in prison with hard labour or worse. When the gang of bal maids from North Roskear Mine was caught red-handed by the mine captain they did not panic or seek to escape without their booty, but instead sought to 'face it out' and defy the official, and if possible escape with their loot. Grace Mayne's defiant attitude and the nerve of Paccoe's daughter in getting a job on the same mine she was fired from the previous day, tell us much about these young women.

Another bal maiden with attitude was Grace Harvey. In July 1823 she stormed into the account house demanding money she said was owed her. *Grace Harvey was here today discoursing very sharply with Enoch concerning some money which she says Enoch owes her.* Harvey

Church Coombe, on the Illogan-Redruth border, looking north toward the main road embankment. A single bal maiden can be seen working the tin slime pits in the valley below Carn Brea Village (Tony Clarke)

Bal maids working in Dolcoath's tin mill beside two convex buddles (Tony Clarke)

showed a total lack of fear for those in authority. She was owed money and she wanted it.

Another type of dishonesty shown by bal maidens came to light in August 1823. Petherick wrote: *If you look over Tom Roger's account, you see what an attempt has been made to impose upon us by Jenny Stone. I knew what she was at altho' I took down the days as she called them over. I've spaled* (fined) *her 5s ... 'Tis a strange thing, that we cannot get correct accounts from them. For my part I'll discharge them as fast as I find them out.* Jenny Stone's dishonest fiddling of the maiden's days was matched by Petherick's outrage.

Other comments by Petherick and Thomas show that flirting between the male workers and the bal maidens was common. Abraham,

BAL MAIDENS ON STRIKE

The 'hungry forties' saw food prices rocket and bal maidens and other poor people suffered. At Devon Great Consols (just east of the Tamar) some 200 young bal maids and lads protested at their low pay rates, asserting that they needed more money to pay for food. Initially, they were successful, but when things improved the mine reduced their wages again. These young ore dressers immediately went on strike, with the result that they were replaced, and when they were taken back on they were paid even less than before. Such confrontations were not unusual, for bal maidens struck work at Dolcoath in 1871, Wheal Basset and Ding Dong mines in 1872 and in Wheal Seton in 1877. These bal maidens rarely won their fights, as there were always other poor people willing to replace them, often for less money. Their actions do tell us, however, that bal maidens were willing to fight, when necessary, for a fair deal.

the chief timberman, who was responsible for ensuring the safety of the shafts and ladderways, appears to have had a notorious relationship with one of the bal maids called Sheaby. It did not stop him flirting with other bal maidens, and his demand for *three weeks round among the women* when he had completed a particularly difficult and dangerous job, was clearly beyond the pale. The two mine captains ribbed him about his demands, and warned him that if Sheaby caught him with any other bal maid *she will put hot lead in his ear*. Another miner, 'Uncle Jack', bragged about being *up all night* with a certain *smart lady*, apparently one of Dolcoath's bal maidens. Another entry has an ore dresser called Enoch singing a romantic song about his most recent conquest among the maidens.

The two captains felt a sense of responsibility toward their maidens. In February 1823 the weather was bad and ore dressing suffered, so that many bal maids were left unemployed. Petherick wrote: *There has been a host of maidens here today, looking for work. I told them we could do nothing for them & they must seek for employ themselves.* He then adds, ruefully, *for if once we begin in that line we shall have our hands full of it every sampling.* He might have felt sorry for them, but if there was no work for them he couldn't take them on. A few days later he says

A group of bal maidens using spalling hammers to break copper ore. The spalling hammer heads were usually between 5–7lb in weight (Henderson)

regretfully, that *Capt Rule gave Penrose orders today to turn off 2 of his maidens.* In March he hoped that ore recently brought to surface would produce *a little work to keep the maidens going,* and again in June, he was anxious to get a damaged shaft repaired so *that we may draw as soon as possible to keep the maidens going.* Petherick and Thomas also liked the bal maidens to enjoy themselves at the local fairs, and there are several comments about seeing them with their boy friends at Camborne and Redruth fairs. Petherick wrote after the Camborne Whit Tuesday Fair of 1823, *There was a great number of our lasses at the fair, some had shiners* (sweethearts) *& some had not. 'Twas a very full fair & the whole passed off without any accidents.* In July Petherick saw some of the bal maidens at Camborne Fair and noted that they had got wet, spoiling some of their finery, to which Thomas replied that he had seen some of them walking home through Troon at about midnight, with some young men. Of course, some of this interest might not have been due to any sense of

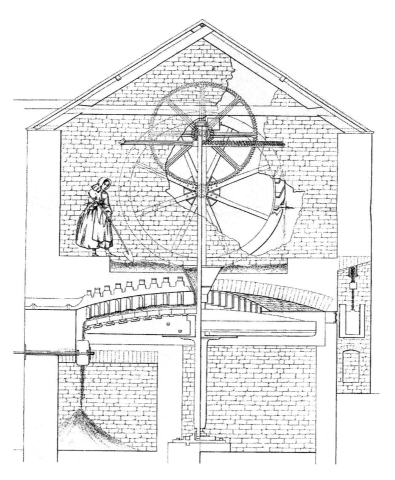

Bal maid feeding ore into the top of a Brunton Calciner. A rotating bed above a furnace enabled the ore to be roasted, releasing arsenic and other sulphides (Henderson)

responsibility, so much as a natural interest in what were probably attractive young girls. Thomas certainly did rib the younger mine captain about his interest in one of these bal maidens – Patience Wills.

In 1841 a Parliamentary Commission was set up to enquire into the employment of children in the mines of Cornwall and Devon. The enquiry was led by Charles Barham. Analysis of these interviews reveals a considerable amount about these workers and evidence of 'coaching' by interested radicals can be seen in the answers given to what were clearly 'leading' questions. The youngest interviewed, Caroline Coom, was only eleven years old. She started at Fowey Consols, as a 'picker', when she was nine years old. The average age that the 21 interviewees started work as bal maids was 12 years. This average was pushed up a little by two of the maidens having started when they were 18 and 20 respectively. Interestingly, Ann Wasley, who worked at Ale & Cakes Mine, said that her five brothers and two sisters started work at the mine when they were 7 or 8 years old. The interviews revealed that, although it was common for the youngest to start as pickers and then move on to cobbing and *carrying* (using hand barrows) as they got older, those who were frail or sick, or who found it too hard, reverted to picking as it was lighter work. Jane Sandow, who worked at Wheal Gorland, and who was 17 worked as a bucker (breaking & crushing ore – considered a *skilled* job), although she thought the work was too hard for her. Elizabeth Karkeek, who was 18, and Sally Fall who was 19 years old, were also employed bucking the ore. Elizabeth Curnow, who worked at Consols, and was aged 24, worked as a cobber, but regularly worked with the samplers, presumably due to her experience. Eliza Allen, who was 20, had only been a bal maid for a couple of years, but due to her ill health and general weakness was employed *sitting down cobbing*. Two 17 year olds, Elizabeth Hockin and Elizabeth Davey were employed *recking* or racking. This task involved the use of an inclined wooden frame to separate small ore from earthy waste.

The various tasks carried out by the bal maids had a variety of effects upon their health and well-being, although the answers these girls gave to clearly 'loaded' questions must have frequently disappointed the investigators. Mary Johns, for example, who was 14 years old and walked 2 miles from her home to Tresavean Mine, said she preferred the mine to working in service, for although it was hard work, she enjoyed better health there. Questioning revealed she suffered back and side pain, especially after carrying the hand barrows for a few hours. She agreed that she often worked outside in wet weather but rarely caught a cold. Grace Bawden, who was 17 years old, and who walked two miles to work, also preferred the mine to her previous employment as a *straw*

Drakewalls Mine, Gunnislake, in the early 20th century. Two bal maidens picking through a huge pile of rock, searching for ore (Tony Clarke)

bonnet maker. She was employed cobbing and spalling and enjoyed her work. Elizabeth Davey, who was 17 years old and employed at Charlestown Mines operating a racking frame, had previously been in service, but much preferred the mine work. This, despite admitting to occasionally catching cold and being described by the examiners as *delicate*. Caroline Coom, the 11 year old, found picking easy and pleasant work, and said it did not tire her. She did admit to getting cold sometimes and had had a fever. She asserted that none of the other pickers complained about the work. Mary Buller's testimony appears to have been unaffected by the nature of the leading questions. She was nearly 16 years old and worked at Fowey Consols as a spaller and cobber, which was quite hard work. She said she enjoyed good health and was not adversely affected by her work. She stated that: *Most of the girls whom I know of, and I know a pretty deal of them in the mine, are strong and hearty.* She did know of one poor girl, who was 18, who was *very weakly*. Mary did reveal one aspect of their work, which is interesting – they sometimes were given work on a 'task and finish' basis – so she sometimes went home at 3 or 3.30pm, instead of the normal 5pm. Mary Ann Rescorle also sometimes worked 'task & finish'.

Undoubtedly, some of the bal maidens suffered physically from their hard labour. Mary Verran, 14, suffered from pain in the back and side although she was only employed as a picker. She also reported that most of the girls she worked with complained about having back pain due to carrying hand barrows. She added that some girls employed as griddlers and spallers had to be sent home due to sickness, especially when they worked outside. Christiana Pascoe, 17, who was employed as a cobber at Consols, said she preferred it to spalling and carrying hand barrows, which tasks had given her a bad back and shortness of breath. The cobbing was done under cover but the other two jobs were performed outside in all weathers. Sally Fall, 19, who worked as a bucker in the Gwennap Mines, complained of palpitations, shortness of breath and pain in her left side, which she attributed to strain from lifting a heavy weight. Christiana Morom, who was 53 years old, and started work in the Gwennap Mines when she was only ten years old, had started to suffer ill-health when she was 33. She had lumbago and had suffered illness and pain for 20 years. Jane Jewell, 21, lasted only a fortnight at Consols, before succumbing to the smell of *mundic water*, which made her feel sick.

One subject about which the investigators showed an interest was the distance these girls walked to work. Mary Verran, who was 14 years old, walked a mile to Gwennap Consols Mine and Elizabeth Curnow, who was 24, walked two miles to the same mine. Jane Sandow, 17, walked three miles to Wheal Gorland. Jane Uren, 16, walked one mile to Tresavean Mine and Mary John, 14, walked two miles to Tresavean. Grace Bawden, 17, walked two miles to Trethellan Mine and Martha Williams, 11, walked two to the same mine. What of the other 14 girls interviewed? Clearly, they all lived within a mile of their work-place, otherwise the reporters would have mentioned it.

The interviews are quite vague on times of starting and finishing work. Only a couple of these bal maidens were clear on when they

Lower Quarter Stamps, Ludgvan, in early 20th century. Posed family group of women. Were any of them bal maidens? Who can say? Good picture of stamps waterwheel (Tony Clarke)

started and when they finished work. Elizabeth Curnow said, when she was 'sampling', she worked from 7 o'clock in the morning till 8 in the evening – a 13 hour shift! Ann Walsey, who was 20 and worked at Ale & Cakes Mine (United), worked from 7am till 5.30pm, with half an hour for dinner – a ten hour day. Mary Buller said that unless she was on 'task & finish' she usually finished work at 5pm. Mary Ann Rescorle, who was 12 and worked at Tresavean, left work at 5.30pm, although she did say she left home for work at 6 o'clock in the morning. Elizabeth Hockin, 17, got up for work at 5.30am, and was back in bed by 9 or 10 o'clock at night. Mary Verran, 14, was up for work between 4.30 and 5am, Christiana Pascoe, 17, was up by 6am and in bed between 10 and 11pm and Martha Williams, 11, said she was in bed by 7 o'clock in the evening.

The education of these girls varied greatly. Some attended village schools before starting work, and most of those continued with their rudimentary education in Sunday Schools once they started work. Of the 21 interviewed only ten could read to some extent. Some read very poorly and others were quite competent. One of their number, Fanny Francis, who was 17 years old and who had been employed at United Mines carrying hand barrows, occasionally taught in a Bible Christian (Bryanite) Sunday School. Nine attended or had attended day school, and most of these continued their education on Sundays in the local chapel Sunday School, which could be Methodist, Baptist or Bryanite. One 12 year old, Mary Ann Rescorle, was taught to read in the workhouse, because her mother could not provide for her. Some of the girls' education consisted of learning to sew and knit and although they could be taught these skills in a 'dame' school, they were also sometimes taught by their mothers at home.

The commissioners were very interested in the diet of these young workers. Martha Williams, 11, testified that she had bread and milk for breakfast, pasty with meat for dinner and tea and potatoes for supper. Mary Verran said she took 'hobban' for dinner, which consisted of plum and potato, although she would have preferred a pasty. For supper she ate fish and potatoes, or stew, roast potatoes or broth. She also said that not many girls had bread and butter with their meals. Jane Uren, 16, who worked at Tresavean, said she drank water with her dinner, and Elizabeth Curnow, 24, employed at Consols, said that the mine had ovens for warming the pasties the girls took for dinner. Some thought the half-hour allowed for dinner was sufficient and others thought it too short.

The wages of these girls varied from mine to mine. The rates paid for different sort of tasks also varied, and as these tasks became harder as the maids got older, so the daily rate tended to increase with age. Seventeen year old Grace Bawden, who was employed cobbing and spalling at Trethellan Mine, was paid 9d a day. Next door, at Tresavean Mine, Elizabeth Karkeek, 18, was paid a shilling a day for bucking 8 barrow loads of ore, which was 12cwt. At Consols, Elizabeth Curnow, 24, was paid 8d a day for cobbing 6 barrow loads (9cwt) of ore. At the same mine Christiana Pascoe, 17, was also paid 8d a day for spalling and carrying 6 barrow loads of ore. Eliza Allen, 20, who was also employed at Consols, was treated considerately. She was allowed to work *sitting down cobbing*, due to weak legs and generally poor health, and was paid 9d a day. Although this amounted to 18s for 24 days, she said she could not normally do half that due to her physical condition.

With the demise of copper mining in most Cornish parishes, in the 1860s, the role of the majority of bal maidens changed dramatically.

Dolcoath Mine, Camborne. Bal maidens can be seen working in the tin mill in the 1890s. They were all quite well-dressed as though they had been warned that they were to be photographed. Convex and concave round buddles were being introduced (Tony Clarke)

From the labour-intensive copper dressing floors of copper mines, these women and girls drifted to the concentrating mills of the remaining tin mines. The dressing of tin required a large volume of water, and so the work of these bal maidens moved for the most part into the valleys which lay close to the large tin mines. Some of the most significant of these mines lay in the parishes of Camborne, Illogan and Redruth. The Red River valley between Camborne and Illogan, had the largest concentration of tin dressing plants in the whole of Cornwall. Between Wheal Grenville and the Basset Mines in the south, and the dressing floors of Dolcoath, Tincroft, Cooks Kitchen, East Pool and South Wheal Crofty, around Tuckingmill, many hundreds of bal maidens were employed in the second half of the nineteenth century – and not just in the tin mills of those mines, but also in the dozens of tailings tin streams which lined the valley between Newton Moor and the sea at Godrevy. At its peak, in the 1870s, over 40 tin streams were operating along the Red River alone. The streams through Pool Village, Carn Brea Village, and Tolgus also were lined with tailings tin streams. With increased mechanisation the number of workers decreased, and women were the first to be laid off, but even by the end of the nineteenth century there were still considerable numbers of bal maidens working in those valleys.

A 19th century drawing of bal maidens at work in a Cornish tin mine. They are working on two batteries of manually operated slime frames for tin dressing (Tony Clarke)

GRACEY BRINEY (1778-1869)

A famous and colourful character who worked as a bal maiden throughout the booms and busts of Cornish copper mining, was Gracey Briney. When she started work in the mines of Redruth in the 1780s the industry was still doing well, but within a short time Gracey was to see the near collapse of local mining and witness widespread hunger, food riots and mobs of miners and soldiers fighting on the streets. She was still working when the industry picked up and boomed after 1800, and she was there to witness its final collapse in the 1860s.

Gracey Briney was born Grace Huchens in Gwennap in 1778 and she lived her early years in the workhouse. She was recruited whilst still a child by Captain Treneer of Treskerby Mine, to work as a surface labourer. One of her first tasks was to lead the horse at the whim, which hauled the ore kibbles up the mine shaft. Bal maidens carrying out this task might not have been as rare as many believe, for on small mines labourers were expected to perform whatever tasks needed doing. As a teenager Gracey became pregnant, although the exact circumstances of this and her subsequent delivery are unknown. One task which was rare if not unique for a bal maiden to carry out was kibble landing. It involved using an iron pot hook to haul the full ore kibble from the mouth of the shaft onto a wooden landing stage, where it was emptied. Not only was the shaft collar exposed to all weathers, but the job required skill, timing and considerable strength and stamina. Although normally a man's job, it was not unknown for a strong bal maiden to do it – and Gracey was just such a women!

Gracey dressed like a man, wore a tall Par Stack hat and hob-nailed boots. She drank with the miners in the Pick & Gad pub at Treskerby, and with her long grey hair and moustache must have looked quite a character. Eventually, Gracey bought her own horse and cart, which she used to carry local produce around the district, and when she started a market stall she drove as far as the Tamar to buy strawberries and cherries to sell there. She also sold fish around the streets of Redruth, for which she was long-remembered.

Gracey Briney was typical of bal maidens over the centuries: tough, independent, resourceful, determined and fearless. When she died aged 91, in 1869, she was widely mourned and greatly missed.

Grace Briney, a famous and formidable bal maiden

THE END OF AN ERA

The census returns for the years 1851 and 1891 show the decline in the number of bal maidens. In the 1851 Camborne Parish returns, for example, there were nearly a thousand women and girls described as working in mines and tin streams. By 1891 this number had dropped to about 520, and although the decrease was dramatic, there was still a large number of bal maids employed along the Red River valley as the century drew to a close. Clearly, if we take into account the neighbouring parishes, the number of women and girls still employed in the tin streams there, would have been considerable.

Few of these tin mills and streaming works have left records of their female employees. However, one small tin stream has left a complete set of records for the years between 1889 and 1894, and again for the years 1911 to 1914. Roscroggan Tin Stream was small by the standards of the time, for although Reskadinnick Tin Stream employed some 300 workers, the Roscroggan works never employed more than 28 in that period. The ratio of male to female workers varied for the five years between 1889 and 1894, with the average being 15 men and boys to 9 women and girls. The works closed in 1894, probably due to the tin price crash, and re-opened in 1911, when the tin price rose. After its re-opening no women and girls are recorded as working there. During the five years (1889-1894) no less than 33 females were employed in the streams, and only two of this number, Elizabeth Williams and Rossina Strauss were employed for the whole five year period. Many of these bal maidens worked for a month or two and moved on. Some came and went during the period, and one or two worked there for periods of up to three years. Elizabeth Williams worked for 10d a day from 1889 to 1894, when, with the fall in the tin price, her rate was lowered to 9d a day. Rossina Strauss appears to have been a girl when she started at the lower rate of 8d a day, and then she received 9d a day until closure. The men earned up to £3 10s a month, on a daily rate of between 2s 3d and 3s 4d, and the boys as little as 15s a month, earning between 1s 2d and 9d a day. In February 1890 there were 16 males and 8 females employed, and of these six girls and nine boys were between the ages of 13 and 18.

Elsewhere on the Red River, bal maidens continued to work well into the twentieth century, and not just in the tailings streams, but also in the tin mills of such mines as Dolcoath. Michael Tangye, in his book *Redruth and its People* (1988), has recorded the memories of Telfer Mitchell, who was born in 1901, and lived his life in the Red River valley. Telfer was a South Crofty miner who, in 1924, was seriously injured in an accident which killed three of his workmates. When he recovered he went to work in the local tin streams, ending his career at Tolgus Tin, as a guide. He recalled that as late as 1915 about a dozen bal maids worked at W G Hocking's Reskadinnick tin streams. *They were all good maidens. They wore a towser* (a sacking apron) *at work and a white apron going to and fro. They didn't wear the gooks then, just a bonnet with a hat pin stuck in it. Some of them was strong, like men, I remember one maiden picked up the boss and thraw'd 'n in in the kieve!* (thrown him into a barrel). *They worked hard, wheeling barrows to the buddles and keeping frames, there was one maiden to each. One of their jobs was 'stankin widths', that is treading heavily on a width of tin stuff that had been through the frames. All the water would then come up from it so that it was pretty dry before it went to the burning-house to*

Geevor Mine, Pendeen, in the 1940s. A young bal maiden tending the shaking tables in Geevor's mill during the Second World War. With so many men in the armed forces women were employed in the mill at Geevor (Paddy Bradley)

take away the arsenic. ... We all had croust together in the croust hut ... One bal maiden worked full time in the croust house, clearing it out and looking after the fire. ... The bal maidens in Dolcoath used to break up the ore stone quite small, about the size of a spoon, using very small hammers with a withy handle, before it went to the stamps. This was done on 'spalling floors'. They were paid by the cubic yard. The bal maidens down Roscroggan earned about 7 shillings a week working 10 hours a day, from 7am until 5.30pm. They had a quarter of an hour croust and half-hour for dinner. The only holidays these bal maidens had, in common with most workers of the time, were Christmas Day, half-a-day for Boxing Day, Good Friday, half of Easter Monday, and Whit-Monday. Telfer said that the last bal maiden he could recall worked at Captain Sammy Williams streams at Tolgarrack, in 1947. She was employed about the croust house there. It is somewhat surprising how similar the working conditions and wages were to those described in the 1841 Barham report. Such things as the working hours, length of time for croust and dinner and holidays were also little changed.

Geevor Mine, Pendeen, in 1946. Possibly the last traditional bal maidens to work in Cornwall. These four girls, Jean Polglase, Stella Oates (Trenoweth), Betty Williams and Phyllis Angove were engaged in picking waste material from a conveyor belt in Geevor's tin mill (Photograph by kind permission of Winnie Sevier, widow of Bill Sevier, the former manager of Geevor)

Perhaps the last bal maidens to be employed on a Cornish mine were at Geevor. Labour shortage during the Second World War led to the management taking on women to work in the mill, and a famous photograph of 1946, reproduced in Cyril Noall's book, *Geevor*, shows four of these maidens 'picking out the waste granite' from a conveyor belt. Jean Polglase, Stella Oates, Betty Williams and Phyllis Angove all look fit, well-fed and healthy, unlike some of the multitude of women and girls who worked so hard for so little over the two previous centuries. Perhaps these really were the last survivors of that vast army of bal maidens who were once such an important and colourful part of the Cornish mining landscape.

What does all this tell us about the Cornish bal maiden? For the most part the evidence shows that they chose their work and enjoyed the comradeship and camaraderie of their workplace. They were not victims, as some modern social historians see them. They were proud of what they were and who they were. We must avoid the danger of generalisations. Examples of dishonesty among those maidens should not lead us to assume that it was common or even widespread. The lewd and outrageous behaviour of some bal maids should not lead us to conclude that such attitudes were the norm. The defiant attitude and disrespect for authority of some of those girls should not make us think that they were all so inclined. The famous or infamous delight of many bal maidens in cheap, bright and colourful clothes, might not have been shared by all their fellow workers. Many of these girls were regular church or chapel-goers, and consequently would not have shared the earthier humour of some of their more outrageous colleagues. What we do know is that most of those bal maidens were young, unmarried and poor. Their meagre wages helped support their families, and any surplus they might have was often spent on cheap clothes and having fun. The evidence shows that they were keen on local fairs, were involved in the many Methodist and other religious revivals and were in every way typical of working women and girls over the centuries who had little, but were determined to enjoy life.

Bibliography

Buckley, Allen, *Hazards & Heroes in Cornish Mines*, 2007,Tor Mark, Redruth

Buckley, Allen, *Princes of the Working Valley*, 2007, Truran Books, Truro

Buckley, Allen, *The Story of Mining in Cornwall*, 2005, Cornwall Editions, Fowey

Burt, Roger (Ed), *Cornish Mining – Essays on Organisation of Cornish Mines & the Cornish Economy*, 1969, David & Charles, Newton Abbot: John Taylor 1814 & 1837; Sir Charles Lemon 1838; Joseph Carne 1839; James Sims 1849

Henwood, George, Ed Roger Burt, *Cornwall's Mines & Miners*, 1972, Bradford Barton, Truro

Jenkin, A K Hamilton, *The Cornish Miner*, 1927, Allen & Unwin, London

Leifchild, J R, *Cornwall, Its Mines & Miners*, 1855, Longmans, London

Mayers, Lynne, *Balmaidens*, 2004, Hypatia Trust, Penzance

Rowe, John, *Cornwall in the Age of the Industrial Revolution*, 1993, Hillside Publications, St Austell

Tangye, Michael, *Redruth & its People*, 1988, Author, Redruth

Tangye, Michael, *Victorian Redruth*, 2001, Author, Redruth